Gateway to Purpose
A Daily Spiritual and Personal Encouragement Guide

Sahran Heslop

GATEWAY TO PURPOSE. Copyright @ 2024. Sahran Heslop. All rights reserved.

No part of this publication may be reproduced, stored in a retrieval system or transmitted in any form or by any means, electronic, mechanical, photocopying, recording or otherwise without the prior written permission of the author.

Published by:

Editor: Cleveland O, McLeish (Author C. Orville McLeish)

ISBN: 978-1-958404-74-4 (Paperback)

DEDICATION

I dedicate this Encouragement Guide to the Holy Spirit, who has helped me tremendously along this writing journey and in my faith walk with God. I stand in total agreement according to John 14:26, "But the Helper, the Holy Spirit, whom the Father will send in My name, He will teach you all things, and bring to your remembrance all things that I said to you." (NKJV). He has done all of the above and so much more for me. I salute You, Holy Spirit.

ACKNOWLEDGMENTS

I must acknowledge and thank my family members who have always believed in me, especially my mom and dad, who have been a tower of strength for as long as I can remember.

To Zanorfa, heartfelt gratitude; you were the first person to encourage me to write this particular book.

To my girls, you have been through many sacrifices with me. May the heavens open over your lives and bless you all.

To my spiritual father, Apostle Courtney McLean, and my spiritual mother, Rev. Nadine McLean; you have both inspired and touched many lives, including mine. I am forever grateful that God has brought me to WAFIF, where you have stirred and provoked the hidden treasures that lie inside me. Thank you, sir, and thank you, first lady. May God continue to use you both to touch the globe for His glory.

To the ministers and colleagues who prophesied over me, calling forth the author; to all of my accountability partners who kept checking on the progress, thank you. As you have poured into my life, may God, our Father, perform many miracles in your life.

Table of Contents

DEDICATION iii
ACKNOWLEDGMENTS v
INTRODUCTION 9
Forgive Easily – DAY 1 11
You Are Being Made – DAY 2 13
Choose to be Motivated! – DAY 3 15
Finding You – DAY 4 17
Positive Meditation – DAY 5 19
The Journey – DAY 6 21
Stay the Course and Partner with God and Others – DAY 7
.... 23
Cry If You Must – DAY 8 25
Make the Step and He Will Make the Provision – DAY 9 .. 27
Trust His hands – DAY 10 29
God's Choice – DAY 11 31
You Are Valuable – DAY 12 33
Self-Talk – DAY 13 35
Do Not Despise the Process; Embrace It – DAY 14 37
You Are a Seed – DAY 15 39
Knowing Your Why – DAY 16 41
Directional Grace – DAY 17 43
Look Ahead – DAY 18... 46

Keep Producing – DAY 19 48
One Word or One Dream – DAY 20 51
Know Your Assignment – DAY 21 53
Faith Over Fear – DAY 22 55
Finding the Balance and Working What Works for You – DAY 23 57
It is In You – DAY 24 59
Purpose is Kicking – DAY 25 61
Clarity – DAY 26 64
Lights On – DAY 27 67
Declare! Declare! – DAY 28 69
Disciples of Christ – DAY 29 71
Focus – DAY 30 73
Conclusion 77

INTRODUCTION

The gateway to overcoming pain and fulfilling your purpose are learned lessons on how to overcome after going through many challenges, discouragements, failures, disappointments, and rejections. These are tools that helped me and were birthed out of my pain—let's just say, my Gateway to Purpose.

This encouragement guide entails daily encouragements, declarations, prayers, the Word of God, and daily activities to propel and stabilize the winner in you.

Results must come after the completion of this encouragement guide. There are things or assignments that God has given you that will be birthed after using this guide.

Forgive Easily | DAY 1

In order to fulfill our purpose in life, we must readily forgive, even when the situation seems too difficult to let go of. Forgiveness is for us, not for those who have hurt us. Unforgiveness will block you from your blessing and God's divine order for your life.

Letting go is a blessing and not a curse; it is an opening that releases access and divine favour.

Scripture: Matthew 6:14-15 (MSG)

"In prayer, there is a connection between what God does and what you do. You can't get forgiveness from God, for instance, without also forgiving others. If you refuse to do your part, you cut yourself off from God's part."

Action Steps:

1. Create a prayer point based on today's encouragement and pray it throughout the day.

___

2. Write down and act upon one task that came to mind as you read today's encouragement.

You Are Being Made | DAY 2

Like grapes needing to be squeezed for wine or olives processed for oil, your potential is maximized through a refining process. Spiritual muscles are being built in you—wait for the flow. Yield to the Master's hand, and what flows from your life will amaze you and those around you.

Life's pressures can be overwhelming, making you feel you can't make it. A while back, I was going through a particular situation, and I heard God's voice saying, 'You are being made.' As I embraced this truth, peace replaced the overwhelming feeling. Though the situation might not have changed immediately, my mindset shifted.

Remember, you are loved by God. It is just a process!

Scripture: 2 Corinthians 4:8-9 (NKJV)
"We are hard-pressed on every side, yet not crushed; perplexed, but not in despair; persecuted, but not forsaken; struck down, but not destroyed."

Action Steps:

1. Create a prayer point based on today's encouragement and pray it throughout the day.

_____

_____

_____

_____

_____

_____

_____

2. Write down and act upon one task that came to mind as you read today's encouragement.

_____

_____

_____

_____

_____

_____

_____

Choose to be Motivated!

DAY 3

Do the challenges, disappointments, and failures motivate or demotivate you?

I really hope you are being motivated!

Keep going. It will be all right; you will win. Failure is in the stopping. I implore you, do not stop!

Obstacles are generally set up to stop or to slow you down. Rest assured, once that obstacle is removed, the opportunity to finish will still be there. What is the use of stopping when you could seek solutions on how to overcome the obstacles? And in doing so, move on, making your way to the finish line.

May every obstacle and challenge back up today. Life is beautiful; make use of and take advantage of every opportunity you get to be better at finishing whatever you have started. I command every garment of discouragement and defeat to leave your life in the powerful name of Jesus.

Scripture: Ecclesiastes 7:8a (NIV)
"The end of a thing is better than its beginning."

Action Steps:
1. Create a prayer point based on today's encouragement and pray it throughout the day.

___

2. Write down and act upon one task that came to mind as you read today's encouragement.

Finding You | DAY 4

I call forth the purpose-driven you that God has destined to impact generations. It is time to discover that person through constant fellowship with the Most High. The world needs you. Rise up and shine brightly; you are the light of the world! God created you uniquely. Be yourself, embrace you! God can only work with the real you.

Scripture: Genesis 32:27 (NIV)
The man asked him, "What is your name?" "Jacob," he answered.

Additional Scripture: Matthew 5:14 (NIV)
"You are the light of the world. A town built on a hill cannot be hidden."

Action Steps:

1. Create a prayer point based on today's encouragement and pray it throughout the day.

_____
_____
_____
_____
_____
_____

2. Write down and act upon one task that came to mind as you read today's encouragement.

_____
_____
_____
_____
_____
_____
_____
_____

Positive Meditation | DAY 5

Check yourself before you wreck yourself!

Negativity can hinder your progress. Whether it is internal or external, no amount of it should stop you. Your mind may not be physically large, but it is one of the largest battlefields. Thousands of thoughts are processed there daily, and these thoughts can either break or build you. Learn to navigate your thoughts and consciously decide to hold on to the positive ones. Before you know it, you will begin to see different results. May your thought process change from this moment onward, in Jesus' mighty name.

Scripture: Philippians 4:8 (KJV)
"Finally, brethren, whatsoever things are true, whatsoever things are honest, whatsoever things are just, whatsoever things are pure, whatsoever things are lovely, whatsoever things are of good report; if there be any virtue, and if there be any praise, think on these things."

Action Steps:

1. Create a prayer point based on today's encouragement and pray it throughout the day.

_____
_____
_____
_____
_____
_____
_____

2. Write down and act upon one task that came to mind as you read today's encouragement.

_____
_____
_____
_____
_____
_____
_____
_____

The Journey | DAY 6

If you are faithful and determined, you will get to your destination.

Do not worry if you have made a few stops and encountered some delays. Rest assured that picking yourself up and starting again brings you one step closer to your destination.

Life is a journey; do not give up, no matter how gloomy it looks. Many success stories would have never been told if the focus had been solely on what the natural eyes beheld. See beyond your eyes. In Jesus' mighty name, may the heart of God towards you be revealed. May the Great You be revealed to you.

Scripture: 2 Corinthians 5:7 (KJV)
"(For we walk by faith, not by sight)."

Additional Scripture: Habakkuk 2:3 (KJV)

"For the vision is yet for an appointed time, but at the end, it shall speak and not lie: though it tarry, wait for it; because it will surely come, it will not tarry."

Action Steps:

1. Create a prayer point based on today's encouragement and pray it throughout the day.

_____
_____
_____
_____
_____

2. Write down and act upon one task that came to mind as you read today's encouragement.

_____
_____
_____
_____
_____
_____

Stay the Course and Partner with God and Others

DAY 7

In life, others will be ahead of you. There is no need to be jealous or compete. Running your individual race is important.

Be patient; you are next in line. Learn to celebrate and support others who are ahead; at some point, you too will be celebrated. Man was created through the partnership of the Father, the Son, and the Holy Ghost. Kingdom warriors arise and unite with your fellow warriors, building the kingdom of God and, by extension, your family, ministry, and business. Even though we are all uniquely different, we still need each other. Let God direct you to your destiny helper in this season.

Reflect on the value of staying the course and partnering with God and others on your journey.

Scripture: Genesis 1:26a (NIV)
"Then God said, 'Let us make mankind in our image, in our likeness.'"

Additional Scripture: James 1:4 (NKJV)
"But let patience have its perfect work, that you may be perfect and complete, lacking nothing."

Action Steps:
1. Create a prayer point based on today's encouragement and pray it throughout the day.

_____

_____

_____

_____

_____

2. Write down and act upon one task that came to mind as you read today's encouragement.

_____

_____

_____

_____

_____

_____

Cry If You Must | DAY 8

Release that which is bottled up inside. It is medicine for the soul. It will not always be tears, but a smile and the oil of joy are right around the corner.

Tears are a language that God understands. God is in control of time and seasons, and His perfect will for your life will manifest. May the endurance power of God rest strongly upon you, and His grace abound with you in this challenging season and always.

Acknowledge and release your emotions, trusting that God understands and will bring joy in due time.

Scripture: Psalm 30:5 (KJV)
"For his anger endureth but a moment; in his favour is life: weeping may endure for a night, but joy cometh in the morning."

Action Steps:

1. Create a prayer point based on today's encouragement and pray it throughout the day.

_____

_____

_____

_____

_____

_____

2. Write down and act upon one task that came to mind as you read today's encouragement.

_____

_____

_____

_____

_____

_____

_____

Make the Step and He Will Make the Provision

DAY 9

There are territories or regions that you have been commissioned to possess.

Let nothing stop you; that territory in the form of a ministry, business, or family is just one step away. God has already spoken, and the blessing is yours; the provisions will line up to your steps. The moment you start to move will be the defining moment, and the universe will respond. After all, God created you, me, and the entire universe. I have tested and proven this strategy. It has worked for me and will work perfectly fine for you. It is really faith and belief. The world has caught on to this, and many Christians are still lagging, not accepting or perceiving who their God truly is and what He is capable of. It is time to arise and access your divine miracle through the power of believing.

Trust that as you take the step, God will make the provision.

Scripture: Psalm 24:1 (NIV)

"The earth is the Lord's, and everything in it, the world, and all who live in it;"

Action Steps:

1. Create a prayer point based on today's encouragement and pray it throughout the day.

_____

_____

_____

_____

_____

2. Write down and act upon one task that came to mind as you read today's encouragement.

_____

_____

_____

_____

_____

_____

_____

Trust His Hands | DAY 10

Remember when He preserved, favoured, and protected you prior to this current situation you are faced with. He has not changed; He remains the same.

Is there anything too hard for God to do? Stay in that place of prayer, worship, and meditating on the Word of God. God's hands are strong.

We often forget past victories, but the most suitable time to reminisce on these victories is when you are in the deepest pits and need to experience the unchanging hand of God. I have experienced close calls on more than one occasion—almost drowning, gunmen showing up to take my life, challenges during childbirth, illnesses, and the list goes on. The same God who was with us through the most horrible situations is still with us. We must trust His hands to guide, deliver, heal, and provide for us.

Let us pause and reflect on one past victory, and through that lens, see your NOW victory. Trust that the same unchanging God will see you through your current situation.

Scripture: Psalm 46:10 (KJV)
"Be still, and know that I am God: I will be exalted among the heathen, I will be exalted in the earth."

Action Steps:
1. Create a prayer point based on today's encouragement and pray it throughout the day.

_____

_____

_____

_____

2. Write down and act upon one task that came to mind as you read today's encouragement.

_____

_____

_____

_____

_____

God's Choice | DAY 11

Rejected by men but chosen by God. A "no" from humankind does not always remain a "no" if the all-powerful God in heaven has said "yes" to you in His Word or by prophecy. Setbacks or delays by no means signify denial. At times, God might just be bringing you into full maturity before the grand reveal of who you truly are to others. Greatness is upon you, and the insurmountable blessings and favour of God.

God sees way beyond what others see; you are God's choice.

Recognize that God's choice overrides the rejection or opinions of men. Trust in God's timing and purpose for your life.

Scripture: Judges 11:1, 2 & 5 (KJV)
Now Jephthah the Gileadite was a mighty man of valor, but he was the son of a harlot; and Gilead begot Jephthah. Gilead's wife bore sons, and when his wife's

sons grew up, they drove Jephthah out, saying, "You shall have no inheritance in our father's house, for you are the son of another woman." And so it was when the people of Ammon made war against Israel, that the elders of Gilead went to get Jephthah from the land of Tob.

Action Steps:

1. Create a prayer point based on today's encouragement and pray it throughout the day.

_____

_____

_____

_____

_____

2. Write down and act upon one task that came to mind as you read today's encouragement.

_____

_____

_____

_____

_____

You Are Valuable | DAY 12

Refuse to settle for less than what you are truly worth.

God values and loves you. I declare that as you acknowledge your true worth, everything that causes you to feel unworthy is broken from your life by the Holy Spirit's power. Every emotional trauma is leaving you now. See yourself above reproach.

Recognize and acknowledge your true worth in God's eyes. Reject any thoughts or influences that devalue you. Embrace the truth that you are priceless to God.

Scripture: Isaiah 43:4a (NIRV)
"You are priceless to me. I love you and honor you."

Action Steps:

1. Create a prayer point based on today's encouragement and pray it throughout the day.

_____
_____
_____
_____
_____
_____

2. Write down and act upon one task that came to mind as you read today's encouragement.

_____
_____
_____
_____
_____
_____
_____

Self-Talk | DAY 13

David encouraged himself in the Lord when all odds were against him. Self-talk is a must. Speaking positively to yourself is a winning tool in the face of negativity, doubt, and discouragement.

"I am good enough."

"It is not my fault."

"The right connection will come."

Practice positive self-talk in challenging situations. Encourage yourself in the Lord.

Scripture: 1 Samuel 30:6 (KJV)

"And David was greatly distressed; for the people spoke of stoning him, because the soul of all the people was grieved, every man for his sons and for his daughters: but David encouraged himself in the Lord his God."

Action Steps:

1. Create a prayer point based on today's encouragement and pray it throughout the day.

_____

_____

_____

_____

_____

_____

2. Write down and act upon one task that came to mind as you read today's encouragement.

_____

_____

_____

_____

_____

_____

_____

Do Not Despise the Process; Embrace It
DAY 14

Embrace the process, knowing that God is at work in you. As you surrender, you will be amazed to see how everything starts to make sense.

In November 2022, I was entrusted with leading a department at my local church. The task seemed overwhelming, and I was on the verge of quitting. Terrified, I sensed God saying, *"Just surrender, and I will help you."* With tears in my eyes, I said yes, and everything shifted. I embraced the process, giving the Author and Finisher of my faith the opportunity to do what only He can do. A year later, I am happy to report that God kept His Word.

Do not run; stand tall on the rock (Jesus) as you are processed.

Acknowledge the process as a means of God working in you. Surrender and trust that He will bring completion to the good work He has started.

Scripture: Philippians 1:6 (NIV)
"Being confident of this, that he who began a good work in you will carry it on to completion until the day of Christ Jesus."

Action Steps:
1. Create a prayer point based on today's encouragement and pray it throughout the day.

_____
_____
_____
_____

2. Write down and act upon one task that came to mind as you read today's encouragement.

_____
_____
_____
_____
_____

You Are a Seed | DAY 15

God planted a seed in you, and within you, there are many seeds. Dying is not an option, for the risk of losing so many other seeds is too great.

I speak life over you. I speak life over your goals and dreams. God's purpose for your life must be established.

Recognize the seeds of potential within you and declare life over your goals and dreams. Embrace the purpose God has planted in you.

> Scripture: Psalm 118:17 (NKJV)
> "I shall not die, but live, and declare the works of the LORD."

Action Steps:

1. Create a prayer point based on today's encouragement and pray it throughout the day.

_____

2. Write down and act upon one task that came to mind as you read today's encouragement.

Knowing Your Why | DAY 16

What is your driving force?

How significant is your why?

Negative experiences should not make you shrink back. Instead, use them as a driving force to perfect a better version of yourself and achieve great success.

Though experiences may tempt bitterness, choose to get better instead.

Identify your driving force and the significance of your purpose. Choose growth over bitterness, using negative experiences as a catalyst for positive change.

Scripture: Jeremiah 29:11 (NIV)
"For I know the plans I have for you," declares the Lord, "plans to prosper you and not to harm you, plans to give you hope and a future."

Action Steps:

1. Create a prayer point based on today's encouragement and pray it throughout the day.

_____

_____

_____

_____

_____

_____

2. Write down and act upon one task that came to mind as you read today's encouragement.

_____

_____

_____

_____

_____

_____

_____

Directional Grace | DAY

17

How do you reach that place where God releases a peace that surpasses human understanding? It begins with acknowledging that, no matter the challenge, God is more than capable of providing help that brings transformation and change.

Towards the end of 2021, during a reflective session, the Lord spoke to me, saying, *"If you had a little more grit, you would have been able to accomplish more this year."* This became my turning point regarding determination. Even when nothing made sense, I kept pushing against suggested thoughts that I would never overcome the situation. I had to defy the odds.

I have come to realize that peace goes beyond simply relaxing and settling the heart; it extends to trusting and believing in God so profoundly that it propels you to move vigorously toward your assignments, defying all odds. This is especially true in areas where no one in your generation has ever conquered or where attempts have been futile.

Acknowledging God's ability to bring transformation and change, even in challenging situations, is the first step toward experiencing His peace that surpasses understanding.

Defying odds is part of your nature, and I declare that you will tap into that in this season of your life.

Scripture: Genesis 12:1 (NIV)

"The Lord had said to Abram, 'Go from your country, your people and your father's household to the land I will show you.'"

Action Steps:

1. Create a prayer point based on today's encouragement and pray it throughout the day.

___

2. Write down and act upon one task that came to mind as you read today's encouragement.

Look Ahead | DAY 18

The past might appear beautiful in the rearview mirror, but trusting and knowing what lies ahead is far better. Upon accepting Christ, many of us may go through a dry season where finances act up and various life challenges arise. Reflecting on the seemingly better days with money, relationships, or possessions is easy. However, it is crucial to keep our eyes fixed on God and the better days ahead, for that is what will manifest.

The journey of faith may lead through challenging seasons, but fixing our eyes on God and anticipating better days ahead is the key to maintaining hope and assurance.

Scripture: Psalm 121:1 (NKJV)
"I will lift up my eyes to the hills from whence comes my help?"

Action Steps:

1. Create a prayer point based on today's encouragement and pray it throughout the day.

_____

_____

_____

_____

_____

_____

2. Write down and act upon one task that came to mind as you read today's encouragement.

_____

_____

_____

_____

_____

_____

_____

Keep Producing | DAY 19

Just like a farmer takes breaks between each crop to clean up and prepare for the next set, as children of God, we are also expected to take breaks, but ultimately, we must return to a state of production. Projects may consume us for a while, necessitating a period of rest, but the crucial part is to come back and resume production.

Between August and December of 2022, a demanding project kept me away from my garden. However, once completed, I happily returned to gardening—cleaning, weeding, and preparing for the next harvest. This cycle does not happen out of compulsion but because I find immense joy and peace in farming. Life's challenges may necessitate breaks, but they should never hinder our growth and productivity.

A sense of peace and overflowing joy consumes me when I am in my garden, especially when I witness the harvest or end results. These crops serve as a clear reminder that nothing is impossible, even if you must take a break and start again. I have faced many adversities throughout my life, but one thing is certain; I have never allowed them to hinder my growth and productivity.

My prayer for you today is that you will envision the end product, maintain laser-sharp focus, and never cease to produce.

Scripture: Matthew 25:16 (KJV)
"Then he that had received the five talents went and traded with the same, and made them other five talents."

Action Steps:

1. Create a prayer point based on today's encouragement and pray it throughout the day.

___

2. Write down and act upon one task that came to mind as you read today's encouragement.

One Word or One Dream

DAY 20

Sometimes, all we need from God is a single word; literally one word. It could also be a solitary dream that brings realignment or refreshment. Personally, in a moment of overwhelming chaos, I distinctly heard the Lord say to me, 'BREATHE,' and that simple directive brought immense peace. While writing this encouragement guide, I experienced something inexplicable. It did not make much sense initially, but within days, a dream brought such clarity that I was astounded by the awesomeness of God.

My prayer for you today is that God will release that one word or grant you a clear dream or vision that brings tranquility to your entire being.

Scripture: Daniel 10:1 (NIV)
"In the third year of Cyrus king of Persia, a revelation was given to Daniel (who was called Belteshazzar). Its message was true and it concerned a great war. The understanding of the message came to him in a vision."

Action Steps:

1. Create a prayer point based on today's encouragement and pray it throughout the day.

_____

_____

_____

_____

_____

_____

2. Write down and act upon one task that came to mind as you read today's encouragement.

_____

_____

_____

_____

_____

_____

_____

Know Your Assignment

DAY 21

In my backyard, callaloo and sorrel plants persistently make their presence felt amidst various seeds that I plant. The lesson here is that each seed is faithfully holding up to its assignment, whether intentionally placed or fallen from a previous plant. The seed understands its mission. Similarly, we must comprehend our assignment to fulfill it.

May your spiritual senses be heightened in this season. I declare over your life that illumination will occur in a matter of days, revealing your assignment for this season.

In the book of Colossians, we encounter Archippus, imprisoned yet fervently praying through the church, understanding and fulfilling his assignment against the odds. Let nothing hinder you from your God-given purpose.

Seeds in the backyard exhibit a lesson in understanding and fulfilling assignments. Archippus, even in prison, prayed through his ministry, emphasizing the importance of unwavering dedication to one's God-given purpose.

Scripture: Colossians 4:17 (KJV)

"And say to Archippus, take heed to the ministry which thou hast received in the Lord, that thou fulfill it."

Action Steps:

1. Create a prayer point based on today's encouragement and pray it throughout the day.

_____

_____

_____

_____

2. Write down and act upon one task that came to mind as you read today's encouragement.

_____

_____

_____

_____

_____

Faith Over Fear | DAY 22

During my time gardening, I marveled at a flower breaking through the concrete pavement. Years ago, carpet grass adorned my yard, but most of it faded away. Yet, traces still lingered, with one grabbing my attention, growing resiliently in the cracks between the fence and the pavement. As mentioned on DAY 21, a few crucial elements become necessary once you understand your mission. Similar to the grass and flowers needing only a bit of soil to thrive, humans also require a small amount of faith to flourish.

Observing the flowers and grass and finding life in unexpected places highlights the resilience that comes with understanding one's mission. As humans, faith becomes our essential soil, allowing us to produce and live purposefully. Strengthening our faith is pivotal in navigating life's challenges and uncertainties.

Today, fortify your faith to lead a meaningful and purposeful life.

Scripture: Hebrews 10:38 (NKJV)

"Now the just shall live by faith: but if any man draws back, my soul shall have no pleasure in him."

Action Steps:
1. Create a prayer point based on today's encouragement and pray it throughout the day.

_____

_____

_____

_____

_____

2. Write down and act upon one task that came to mind as you read today's encouragement.

_____

_____

_____

_____

_____

_____

Finding the Balance and Working What Works for You

DAY 23

People are at various stages in their journeys, and there is no need to compete with anyone. Find your niche, keep working on it, and simultaneously focus on self-development. Do what brings you joy and peace, and remember to persevere even when challenges arise. In mentoring Timothy, Paul emphasized the importance of not being swayed by others' opinions and highlighted self-development as a crucial factor that eliminates unnecessary competition.

Different individuals are on diverse paths, and each person's journey is unique. The emphasis is on finding your niche, working on it consistently, and concurrently investing in personal growth. Paul's mentoring of Timothy serves as a reminder that seeking guidance and focusing on self-development are vital components in unleashing one's full potential.

Scripture: 1 Timothy 4:12-14 (NIV)

"Don't let anyone look down on you because you are young, but set an example for the believers in speech, in conduct, in love, in faith and in purity. Until I come, devote yourself to the public reading of Scripture, to preaching and to teaching. Do not neglect your gift, which was given you through prophecy when the body of elders laid their hands on you."

Action Steps:

1. Create a prayer point based on today's encouragement and pray it throughout the day.

   _____
   _____
   _____
   _____

2. Write down and act upon one task that came to mind as you read today's encouragement.

   _____
   _____
   _____
   _____
   _____

It is In You | DAY 24

The key to unlocking your dreams or goals is already within you!

No force can extinguish your dreams but yourself. God has granted you the key to access what He placed inside you. Decide not to self-sabotage. While it is crucial to recognize and combat opposing forces, the Bible encourages us to bind, cancel, or rebuke and call forth what we desire.

Take a moment to reflect: *Are you spending more time binding than calling forth?* Take note of your actionable steps toward your goal. As your mindset shifts and you start speaking things into existence, be prepared for the acceleration that will manifest in your life.

Scripture: Matthew 18:18 (NIV)
"Truly I tell you, whatever you bind on earth will be bound in heaven, and whatever you loose on earth will be loosed in heaven."

Action Steps:

1. Create a prayer point based on today's encouragement and pray it throughout the day.

_____

_____

_____

_____

_____

_____

_____

2. Write down and act upon one task that came to mind as you read today's encouragement.

_____

_____

_____

_____

_____

_____

_____

Purpose is Kicking

DAY 25

Feeling restless, sensing that there is more to your life than your current experience? If so, what steps have you taken to address it?

We sometimes find ourselves lagging behind God's timetable for our lives. God is aware of it, and we often sense it too. This can lead to unexplainable frustration and a lack of peace or comfort because purpose is stirring within you. During these times, prayer becomes crucial. The Lord, through prayer, releases directional grace upon you. It is possible that repentance is needed for not fully embracing what God has asked you to do due to various constraints. Many lives may depend on your 'yes.' Surrender to God; say 'yes' and free yourself from frustration.

I recall a period when God persistently impressed upon me the need to write. It was a challenging time, and frustration was an understatement. I vividly remember the Lord saying, *"Unless you obey Me, this feeling will not leave you."* Once I obeyed, the frustration lifted, and as I write this, I am filled with joy. It is essential to remember that we can never outsmart God. Embracing the challenge and pleasing God is the better path.

If you feel the kick of purpose within you, do not resist. Embrace it, for it is a call to align with God's plan. Take time in prayer, seek direction, and be willing to say 'yes' to what God has placed in your heart. The fulfillment of purpose brings lasting peace and joy.

Scripture: Isaiah 43:1 (KJV)

"But now thus saith the Lord that created thee, O Jacob, and he that formed thee, O Israel, Fear not: for I have redeemed thee, I have called thee by thy name; thou art mine."

Action Steps:

1. Create a prayer point based on today's encouragement and pray it throughout the day.

_____

_____

_____

_____

_____

_____

2. Write down and act upon one task that came to mind as you read today's encouragement.

_____

_____

_____

_____

_____

_____

_____

Clarity | DAY
26

Are you weary from consistently making the wrong choices and finding your judgment clouded? I have been there, too, until I shifted my gaze towards Jesus. At that moment, I found that my judgment improved, and decision-making became much clearer.

I consistently impart this wisdom to my children and those around me: it is always better to speak the truth than to resort to lies. People often compromise when they feel cornered, unable to see an alternative. I have discovered that maintaining clarity and integrity has preceded many of the favours I have received. Take, for instance, navigating customs at the airport, faced with specific questions where an honest "yes" could easily lead to extra charges. Despite the potential consequences, my response remains an honest "yes," and more often than not, it is followed by favour. I shudder to think of the outcomes had I chosen dishonesty.

The question may arise, *"How did I get here?"* The answer lies in my daily growing relationship with God. The closer I draw to Him, the more clarity I experience, elevating my level of conviction.

If you still cannot move past your mistakes and failures, there is still hope. Submit them, along with your heart, fully to God. Just as God has delivered me, I declare that clarity is breaking through for you now. May the liberating power of God descend upon you. I speak over your life: you are released from every wrong choice, and your transformation begins now.

Scripture: Genesis 12:11-13 (NIV)

"As he was about to enter Egypt, he said to his wife Sarai, "I know what a beautiful woman you are. When the Egyptians see you, they will say, 'This is his wife.' Then they will kill me but will let you live. Say you are my sister, so that I will be treated well for your sake and my life will be spared because of you.""

Action Steps:

1. Create a prayer point based on today's encouragement and pray it throughout the day.

_____

_____

_____

_____

_____

_____

2. Write down and act upon one task that came to mind as you read today's encouragement.

_____

_____

_____

_____

_____

_____

_____

Lights On | DAY 27

Walking with God automatically makes you a beacon of light, and in a world that yearns for illumination, our role as carriers of divine light is more crucial than ever.

Self-Reflection: What is Your Status?

If your light is fully shining, it indicates that God has your heart. If not, draw closer to Him, for He is the Father of light. As God's children, we carry His light, radiating it wherever we go. This radiance is not confined to religious attire—*do I dress religiously in long skirts and hats, etc.?* The answer is no. In fact, a fellow sister in the Lord has a restaurant. Every time I go there, one of her employees calls me the "mystery lady." She conveyed that I am always looking different, but one thing that is always evident is the glow I carry.

A personal encounter—like being dubbed the "mystery lady" in a restaurant—should reveal a distinctiveness, a luminosity that speaks of a divine connection. As born-again believers living a successful Christian life, our exterior must reflect the transformation happening within our soul. Those around us should sense that we are God's children without the need for verbal confirmation. This radiant glow has the power to draw others closer to both you and God. May your destiny helpers be guided to you because of the light you carry, in Jesus' name.

Scripture: Matthew 5:14 (NIV)
"You are the light of the world. A town built on a hill cannot be hidden."

Action Steps:
1. Create a prayer point based on today's encouragement and pray it throughout the day.

_____

_____

_____

2. Write down and act upon one task that came to mind as you read today's encouragement.

_____

_____

_____

_____

Declare! Declare! | DAY 28

My prophecy will not always remain a prophecy; I will push towards making it a reality from the spirit realm to the earthly realm.

For years, I sensed the need to upgrade my vehicle, but I hesitated to move. It continued until I received a word. In the middle of receiving the word, a doubtful thought came upon me, and God rebuked me. The rebuke was so strong that it straightened me up, and I started moving towards God's words. Many times, we receive a word, but the action does not line up, causing delays in what God wants to do in our lives. Throughout the entire process of acquiring the vehicle, I had to declare God's words and wait for the manifestation. In the middle of the pandemic, I received my brand-new car through prophecy and declarations.

Declaration is a powerful thing. It is your time to make your own declarations. Many people have made their decrees over your life, and it is now time for you to overrule them.

Scripture: Job 22:28 (NKJV)

"You will also declare a thing, and it will be established for you."

Action Steps:
1. Create a prayer point based on today's encouragement and pray it throughout the day.

_____

_____

_____

_____

_____

2. Write down and act upon one task that came to mind as you read today's encouragement.

_____

_____

_____

_____

_____

Disciples of Christ | DAY 29

Following Christ's example to obey the Father's command grants us access to the heart of God.

Are you a true disciple of the Lord? Reflect on your actions; are there ways you have contradicted the Lord's commands?

Access will be granted, and the benefits He has promised will flow exponentially if one becomes yielded. It is time to yield; He requires that from you now more than ever.

Scripture: John 15:10 (NIV)
"If you keep my commands, you will remain in my love, just as I have kept my Father's commands and remain in his love."

Additional Scripture: Psalm 103:2 (KJV)
"Bless the LORD, O my soul, and forget not all his benefits."

Action Steps:

1. Create a prayer point based on today's encouragement and pray it throughout the day.

2. Write down and act upon one task that came to mind as you read today's encouragement.

Focus | DAY

30

When you have wavered long enough and finally pushed past that phase in your life, it is now time to focus. To truly focus, one must make a conscious decision to shut out anything or anyone that will affect their energy negatively. In labor, a mother has one aim—to safely bring forth a child. Nothing else truly matters during labor and delivery.

I declare that God will be the center of your delivery moment, along with the chosen few He will use to aid in the process. It is time to push that baby out—your gateway to purpose. It will take laser-sharp focus, shutting out everything and anyone that will distract you.

Sanballat and Tobiah ridiculed the Jews who were rebuilding the walls of Jerusalem. The Jews did not allow distraction to stop them; they continued with great focus. The walls were rebuilt, and even so, their enemies still plotted. Remember, your focus is your responsibility; your enemies know their responsibility, and so should you.

Scripture: Nehemiah 4:6-9 (NIV)

"So, we rebuilt the wall till all of it reached half its height, for the people worked with all their heart. But when Sanballat, Tobiah, the Arabs, the Ammonites, and the people of Ashdod heard that the repairs to Jerusalem's walls had gone ahead and that the gaps were being closed, they were very angry. They all plotted together to come and fight against Jerusalem and stir up trouble against it. But we prayed to our God and posted a guard day and night to meet this threat."

Action Steps:
1. Create a prayer point based on today's encouragement and pray it throughout the day.

2. Write down and act upon one task that came to mind as you read today's encouragement.

_____

_____

_____

_____

_____

_____

_____

_____

Conclusion

As I was able to birth this encouragement guide, I declare that you will birth and release everything that God has placed in the womb of your spirit. Nations are waiting for your 'yes.'

My charge to you is that nothing is impossible; there is always a way out.

LET THE NEXT CHAPTER BEGIN: PURPOSE ON THE HORIZON

Made in the USA
Columbia, SC
14 March 2024